Poetic Prose

Jane Alise Lenzen

To order additional copies of this book, contact:
Xlibris
844-714-8691
www.Xlibris.com
Orders@Xlibris.com

ISBN: 978-1-6698-4081-7 (sc)
ISBN: 978-1-6698-4082-4 (hc)
ISBN: 978-1-6698-4080-0 (e)

Library of Congress Control Number: 2022914105

Print information available on the last page

Rev. date: 08/17/2022

CONTENTS

Introduction

With a life long love of learning, curiosity will often take many of us on a journey towards a glimpse of what makes various things tick, such as people, animals, nature, galaxies and unseen forces.

As a bird takes flight to soar in the sky like a raptor, forage for food to feed her brood or enjoy the colony of friends, it knows it has a place in this world; one that is meaningful and abiding. Isn't that what we all want?

My poetic prose, both serious and whimsical, are a small component of many life long ponderings. For 25 years I wrote a column I titled "Words to Ponder," in a North Georgia newspaper utilizing ideas from well known philosophers, psychologists, artists, authors, scientists, and religious or political leaders. I would occasionally use my own musings anonymously just for the fun of it which would sometimes evoke positive letters to the editor, generating, for me, a big smile.

Everyone wakes up each day immediately connecting their inner world with the outer. Poets enjoy distilling these connections, putting their own personal slant on observations then allowing words to flow without much deliberate concentration.

As life progresses, perspectives and conclusions develop either consciously or unconsciously. Some of us have to write about them, others don't. Either way, we all add to this glorious mix which keeps our world interesting and worth studying.

In my 70 plus years I've noticed that education makes little difference in our day to day insights, how eloquently we express ourselves or what kinds of mental dispute resolutions we use to get along in our society. I, for example, have a B.A in Psychology and Graduate degrees in Clinical Nutrition and Gerontology, but cannot do mathematical equations in my head or forecast the weather by simply observing various types of cloud formations as some can. I have known many people with High School degrees or less who are far more brilliant and interesting than many of us with advanced degrees. No matter what our background is or where our interests lie we all have a splendid story to tell and poetry residing within us.

We live in a world of change and adaptation with so much to do in the way of improving it. It's important to take the time to see the big picture in a kind of gestalt manner and notice the impact that we have on others and our environment.

These ponderings to follow are part of that process. Read them slowly and then reread a couple more times. I must do this with other poets as some leave me scratching my head which you will experience with a few of mine and that's OK. Seldom are there obvious conclusions or common themes, just streams of thoughts (with some research thrown in) tied together by a bundle of words that hopefully make a fairly solid statement.

I genuinely thank you for taking the time to read them.

Jane Alise Lenzen

Theology

By Jane A Lenzen

Religions reach for the Divine
Belief systems, rituals, dogma
Bondage to ideas and creeds
Truth to some, fiction to others.
Keep the path narrow
Do not stray from virtuous goals.
Focus on salvation and faith
Compliance, no matter the pain
Black, white, absolute
Brings joy to some, confusion to others.

The web of life unites-
Inseparable from universals.
No exclusion from other.
Permeating principles reign,
Not unlike quantum illusion.
Finding meaning in struggle.
Steadfast syncretism

Value the big picture
Know where you stand
Without wavering, yet
Judging all kindly

Relentless passions agree
Knowing what little you know
Observing and listening
Taking comfort in the search.
A greater cause than self
Reveals ancient wisdom.
Collectivist positions melt into
Devotion to an inner life.

Embodied in reasonable theologies
Find comfort in abstract or gray areas
Listen to circadian and tribal lessons.

Cooperation and mercy reign
Emanating light from the soul
Pursuing the divine spark
Where all is good, all is God.
It can be nothing else.

Grateful

By Jane A Lenzen

Human devouring desires can bring
Misery to those who yearn for comfort.
Wanting no pain unconsoled,
Man does most anything to obtain
Ease and smooth sailing.

We tremble at major roadblocks
Expecting a clearing ASAP
Until a sudden thought rivets the mind:
What if I chose calm and listened
To another tune in my head instead.

When stubbing a toe, consider the fact
That your toe still remains on your foot!
When seemingly held down by force
Take flight on gleaming wings and
Shine through dark moments.
Be grateful that the mind is able to
Converse with itself and hear
Another more soothing conversation.

Gratefulness practiced daily
Diminishes the existential threat
Of living a lie to make things "right."
It's as if you collaborate with yourself
By adding just enough pluses to
Wipe out just enough negatives.....
Making life worth all the inevitable trouble
That's bound to come your way,
Again, again and again.
And when the next again comes knockin'
A grateful heart says,
"Oh, it's you once more. Come on in
And sit awhile. You are welcome to be
My teacher as your difficult task
Makes me stronger.
And for this I am grateful."

10 MINUTE OBSERVATION

By Jane A Lenzen

Nature's contrast everywhere
Palm branches flow while
A lizard observes me
In a coevolutionary manner.

Orange flowers flow
To greet my eager green eyes
Oh! The colors tease me so
To paint a picture of this unique moment.

An ant crosses a stem
To a place unknown to me
Of which I'd love to travel
On long stalks in tandem.

The bark speaks to me
Of ages long ago.
With moss clinging tightly to a
Long awaited story.

I will be still just long enough to
Listen to the tale of this tiny universe.
Ten minutes today, twenty tomorrow.

Native Ways

By Jane A Lenzen

Medicine Man, I seek your presence
Red Man, Red Woman, heal my pain.
Lay hands on me, chant your prayer
Breathe deep of sacred pipe and fire
Burning herbs with holy sparks lift
My soul in annual festival of wild dance.

Turtle shell and gourd rattlers
Drums of hemlock and buckeye
Rhythmical movement of ecstasy.
Before selfishness entered the world
Sharing with all was the norm
The revered Great Spirit was pleased.

Fun with marbles, butterbeans,
Sticks and discs.
Competition fiercely fun,
Real battles can wait
Hunting for food put off for now
Wild plants and animals spared
Lambsquarters, berries, Buffalo, cress,
Nuts, deer, vegetables,
Sassafras and insects relax
When teasing laughter continues.

Canoes carved of poplar, homes of oak
Furniture of chestnut, straw mattresses
Cushiony soft.
Cane baskets woven
And dyed to *agehya's* taste.
Rooms lit with Mullein leaves
Dipped in grease clear evil spirits.
Friendships deepen, stories embellished,
Until weariness sets in for
Cherished sleep. *Osda enoyi.*

Sunrise beckons eyes to open,
The dream fades to view
The awakening hot yellow star.

Boredom nonexistent in this tribe
Cooperation and collaboration
Led to basic ease of survival
As long as natural instincts
Were adhered to daily.
The earth fed and clothed them well
Reciprocated with respect for its
Great Goodness
Generosity begat generosity
And so it went, until the white man....

Mystical Mystery Tour

By Jane A Lenzen

Believing in a Superior some thing or ONE
Feels contrite and elemental when others
describe what's Intuitively known.

Different versions taught for millennia to
faithful masses take hold for awhile
Yet deep within we may recognize our
Knowledge is minuscule concerning the
Nonlinear Creator of massive Universes.

Beliefs in a specific or nuanced concept
of God is not necessary if we instinctively
know One exists.
Isn't this enough?
That ineffable, alive, innate validity that
This Great Power is obvious, everywhere
and accessible beyond what's visible.
Souls connect regardless of recognition.

Reality of Space tempts the cells to grab
hold of this Divine Spark.
Unfathomable experiences that only last
seconds, can impress into perpetuity.

Spiritual exploration began when man took
his First Breath.
Biblical characters from Judaism and others
describe both simple and complicated lives
where cries were heard by a Single God
who always obliged.

Christianity and Islam bounced off Hebrew
texts with their own take on these stories
describing an unwavering faith invulnerable
to historical writings.

Buddhists, Taoists, Hindus, Confucians,
Sikhs, Baha'ians, Zoroastrians, Jains, just to
name a few, want to live in a society with
rules and ideas which keep the masses on
track, by improving a relationship with this
outward or inward Being of Light.

I wonder what the Creator, who abides in
Every Thing thinks about all this.
Then again,
God, with many names, probably has little
to think about since
Imperishable "Being," not circumstances,
is more relevant than processing countless
Duplicitous thoughts.

The endowment of each creature with
Sacred Understanding from birth means
little must be taught about that which is
already sensed; life itself is a
Mystical Mystery Tour
which seems radically familiar once
Awakening takes place.

We simply allow each Holy Moment to
unfold in its most natural state and relish
the beauty residing in Wise Narratives.

So the next time you hear a bird sing, sing
back and it will listen.
This bird and you will have shared Holiness.

Death can't separate you either;
from Dust you came and to Soil shall
you return, nourishing both plants and
earthworms who then feed
baby birds who then
sing a duet with the Next Generation
where recycled Souls live on and on.

This Magical Mystical Mystery never dies.

The River Flow

By Jane A Lenzen

River quickly flows to softening rocks
Meandering, volatile and substantial
This determined downhill march
Unclogs the depth of memory

Keep me flowing like this river.

Watching trees go swiftly by
Waving leaves demand attention
The river roar soothes its branches
Bubbling ripples spiral unfazed

Keep me flowing like this river.

Broken branches from a storm
Each bowing to a glorious current
Rushing to its next destination
At a pulling pace consistent

Keep me flowing like this river.

A frozen moment like heavy gravel
Must yield to the gorge
Opening my stagnant mind
To nourishing layers of delta

Keep me flowing like this river.

Let the waterfall grant me mercy
The cascade, cleanse my spirit
Overflowing banks soothe my soul
Oh! This ephemeral moment will

Keep me flowing like this river.

A Priori

By Jane A Lenzen

Consummate reflections accepted
Brilliant oracles received

Before understanding,
Your Inner World already knew

The content of empirical experience
Ushers in unpredictable truths
Beyond analyzing concepts

The nature of thoughts
May be devious, loving, most illusionary
Acts are judged harsh or kind
What do we know of another?
Stories we make up
Deny truth of our and others' interior
That Deeper State of Knowing

This Ground of Being
The intuition from birth
Is all that is sincerely real

To want something to be
Not what it is
Demands unnecessary energy
Zaps momentary awakening

Rest in knowing that you know
Just enough that's important

Not what you envision or hear
But a simpler sense of seeing
The way things present
Without toil and angst
Reacting and examining, instead
Being with *a priori* from the womb
Allowing basic self to unfold
A transcendent sense of wonder that's
Neither truth nor knowledge
Rather a connection to environment
As it is versus what it should be

Every moment offers newness
Engulfing one with a priori that
Surpasses all perceived notions

Signals from your personal antenna
Become refined through a
Language that is all your own

Mental "Illness"

By Jane A Lenzen

What is insanity to some
Is brilliance to others
Perceived as reality to one
Is delusional to another.

What factors define a neurosis?
Articulations, IQ, social norms
With various aberrations and quirks?
DNA curses may simply equate to
Misunderstood personalities.

Verbalizations within the mind
May seem like ignited lightening to one
And soft fleece to another.
Language differs from species to species
Human to human, chimp to chimp.
No two beings are alike.

Hormones, nature, nurture, germs, diet
All entertaining ideas, easy to blame.
The power of pharmacy improves some,
Confusing others with dead Delta waves,
Whipping a tired horse during a race.

Experiences mold a baby's brain whose
Biological makeup may cancel out
Any Tenderness bestowed.
Cold responses to touch disturb a parent
So willing to shower with love.
Neglect, on the other hand, is far worse.
Prosaic attention creates mental despair.
The growing child becomes an outcast,
Possibly a bully or worse, a criminal.

Many illnesses of the mind are
Perceptions of experts poised to put
Convenient Labels upon the innocent.

Like a Golem, the "patient" fights for a life
beyond clay images.
A life that may be better understood
Outside the boundaries of convention and
appearances....

And if seen with reassuring eyes by
Someone who Peeks into their Soul,
allowing the golem to
Speak a language where they may, with
Understanding, be Heard, then
"The afflicted " can enter into a
Threshold of Rebirth and
This, my friend, is a genuine Gift for both.

Gentle Giants

By Jane A Lenzen

Feeling appropriately small
In the midst of the vast universe
We dream of our heritage,
Discovering that Mammoth behavior
Paved the way for tiny organisms and
Humans to evolve into plenty.

These behemoth beauties are inextricably
Linked to our long lineage of lessons.
Their presence, like the Blue Whale,
Shows complexity and mystery
Not unlike the human animal itself,
Maybe more.

Their instinctive processes allow
Cooperative social relationships,
Dependent on clan movement.
Memories cannot be erased
With their dead, long mourned.

Like other non human animals
Elephants' empathy for others
Easily suggests that
Emotions run profoundly deep
Love has no limits, sparking
A mosaic of emotional intelligence.

Vocalization frequencies tell
Stories that only the species understands.
Seismic refinements make for
Amazing awareness not understood by
The human mind, who may view them as
Ivory or silly circus acts, belying the
Psyche of fierce yet tender creatures who
Give counsel to the utmost worldly.

These Gentle Giants who live on either the
Savannah or forest, form Matriarchal
Bonds, caring for each others' offspring,
who learn the willful ways of their herd.

A 50 mile stretch doesn't detract from
Communicating with each other.
The altruistic bond between them is
A trait humans can effectively emulate.
Our prayer to the heavens could well be:
"Mold me to be more like an elephant"
and if your wish is granted, what a
wonderful friend you would turn out to be.

Joie de Vivre

By Jane A Lenzen

Happiness as a concept means
Various things to different people.
What brings joy to one may
Sling arrows at another.

Some ride in hot air balloons
To staggering heights
While others prefer terra firma
Up close and personal.

Some kill animals for fun or trophy
While others admire them from afar
Enjoying sweet moments of bliss.

Gladiators of old brought
Cheers and laughter against beasts.
Today dogs or chickens are pitted
Against one another for excitement
While others mourn their pain.

In unambiguous terms we see that
One man's smile is another's frown.
The embodiment of dual natures
Reside in each one of us.

A simple joke sidesplitting to one
Is crude, evoking a wince to another.
One man's expensive vacation is
A vain extravagance to a friend.

Recognition and prize feeds one ego
While another shuns the spotlight,
Finding peace and pleasure in solitude.
Riding the rapids is riveting to one
A need for resuscitation for another.

Sophisticated intellectuals love knowledge
Simpler minds content in dull days.
Some get high from rolling of the dice
Others cringe at the loss of a dollar bill.

Supreme ecstasy with head in clouds,
To another, dark silent exile
In a cavernous chasm.

What is Joie de Vivre to the goose may not
be so grand for the gander.

GOD's Opinion

By Jane A Lenzen

We humans have our opinions and
God has another.
Humans create God in our image while
God is God without human input.
Humans want God to be compliant;
God is not concerned with trivialities.
Humans cry out when life is tough,
Yet often inconsequential.
Humans want God to intervene but
Everything has already been given.

God's opinion feels beyond our reach
Human brains can't scour divine depth.
God goes in one direction
Humans another.
We wrap ourselves in a blanket of
Armor, waiting for reckoned relief.

Once, however, we settle into "what is"
God's opinion trickles down
Touching minds with spiritual presence.
Once in alignment, God moves in
Mysterious Ways toward our instincts,
Like a dog chasing a scent.
Once on this trail, there is no turning back;
You know the direction and
God's opinion is in plain sight.
It is then that we become God's hands;
With moral muscles flexed,
Where we, in turn, help others who
Cannot help themselves.

Smiling, God nods in approval.

On a lighter note…since we share
Ancestral roots with the Great Ape,
Maybe these Magnificent Creatures
Have similar concerns about the
Opinions of their Maker.
And if they create God in their own
Image, as do we, then God may have
To change opinions depending on the
Ape or human centric lens.

So maybe God entrusted to everyone
The idea that the heavens open up
When acceptance and kindness reign
This is not an opinion
But a Law that God made sure
Worked for everyone and everything.

Now dogs and cats may have an entirely
Different opinion about God.
Dogs only see God's tail wag and a treat,
Which greatly amuses God's senses.
And Cats, well, they walk the other way,
mumbling under their breath,
"Who cares about God's opinion….."

Everything Has Meaning

By Jane A Lenzen

The purpose of all life seems
Concealed under a canopy.
Like Bumble Bees who never question
Orders from the Queen,
Follow Bee society rules since
Their actions make for a pleasant life.
Humans are not all that different
They, too, find meaning in social order.

Sometimes life's explanations manifest
Like a flash of lightening
Then quickly hide again
Enticing the mind to keep searching,
Why so much suffering is mingled with joy.

We may feel at the mercy of
The next storm coming our way.
Perplexed hearts ask why,
While others bravely trudge through.

Elated moments return to
Caress the almost broken spirit.
Clarity unfolds and reverberates
Loudly, then to an imperceptible tune.

The background of meaning murmurs,
Luring the heart back into the game,
Ready to take on the next fight where
The wrestling gets easier
And the burdens lighter.

Meaning is in it all,
Ready to be savored
Moment by moment, breath by breath,
Encompassing the worst and best
That life and all its handiworks
Have to offer.

The Cosmic Web

By Jane A Lenzen

Embedded in the universe is harmony
Singing in the wind as if to say,
We are in partnership by
Observing and creating each other.
We share the same molecules
Recognizable narratives
A similar covenant
Among our 100 trillion
Neural connections
And 100 billion faraway galaxies.

The universe reaches out its arms
To enfold the entire system of matter,
An umbilical cord impossible to cut.

Stars birthing all with like elements
Teaching us lessons about
the dependable vastness of life,
Being utterly indifferent to
most situations we deem difficult;
Viewing our predicaments
In a more virtuous light,
No need for lamentations
When most earthly problems are
Caused by earth beings.
All preventable predicaments
If first we had listened to the stars.

The unity of the world circulates within.
Life begets life through deep intuition
Of vast connections to all.
Separation is impossible, like quarks,
Never found in isolation.

Nothing can escape
The Fabric of Life's Forces,
Like cosmic rays penetrating every thing.
Strange and charming energy felt by all,
Yet the phenomena is seldom realized.

Once awakened, integrative mysteries
Come alive and
Fundamental Entanglement
Forevermore grants us a peek into
Extra ordinary endless possibilities,
All because we gave up the silly idea of
Being separate.

Equality

By Jane A Lenzen

Who is our brother and sister?
Does DNA define our relatives?
Where do our thoughts roam
When burning mental movies of
Youth, where innocent minds
Were fascinated with
Uniqueness In others
Until taught differently by adults.

Some may be convinced that red apples
Are superior to green.
By taking someone else's word for it
These "inferior" green ones will be
Overlooked in the store, ignored since
It's a "well-known fact" that any green
Apple is not worth "getting to know"
On a personal level.
This is how prejudice works and yes,
It's just that absurd.
We can fertilize our emotions
Be grateful for the differences...
This world made up of beautiful and various cultures and hues of skin color-
Exploitation cannot be welcome within the human heart or neighborhood,
Everyone's success is dependent on
Connectedness.

Mental anesthesia of past injustices make way for new ones.
Each is responsible for creating a world worth living in, not for a few
but for everyone.

31

Tree Climb

By Jane A Lenzen

Looking upward, studying the canopy
I see the perfect tree, draped with moss
and air plants, ready for company.
One big leap I latch onto a strong branch,
My legs sway upward to catch a limb.
Climbing continues to a high rest stop.

What a view! Neighborhood kids
Skipping rope and
Cars racing on an
Uncrowded street. What's the hurry?
Come join me aboard this mighty tree
Feel the breeze flow around branches
That no convertible can match.

The squirrels, used to my presence,
Continue to play with each other.
I want to be as quick in my climb
But my four limbs won't scurry as well.
Atop, the bending limb says BE CAREFUL!

Easing my way down I see the squirrels
Holding their breath in suspense.
Will the little girl make it down this time?
She sure seems unsteady.

The closest limb to the ground appears
Much higher now.
How did I get up here so easily?
Where to jump to avoid protruding roots?
My shins still hurt from the last mishap.
Maybe I'll stay a little longer in this refuge
I feel like King of the mountain.

Hunger begins to set in.
I must take a leap of faith to get home.
There are plenty of other trees to climb
Not quite as high but every bit as alluring.
Soaring down, my feet hit hard and I roll.

I look back at this sturdy hardwood and
Promise to return soon with more
Tales of adventure.

I yearn to know its history, all it has
Witnessed over the years.
Birds will sing to me a descriptive
Tune that spin a tale of centuries past.

Climbing any tree, one realizes that we
Also began as a tiny seed, miraculously
Progressing to maturity.
The symbiotic attraction of child to tree
Never leaves once both become adults.

When I die, I hope to return as an
Egg in a nest of this very tree.
Once bursting out of my shell
I will gaze at the bark and leaves and say,
Ah, yes, I am finally back home.

Desert Stones

By Jane A Lenzen

The dawning sun sits low in the sky
To greet dry brittle bones.
Yet among them are the living,
Enduring expected challenges while
Awaiting the rainy season of renewal

Until then, parched throats do not
Prevent the enjoyment of a white dawn.
Dromedary camels with big brown eyes
View the landscape of the endless
Desert stones with pleasure
While their small ears
Amplify the tiniest of sounds.

The Fennec Fox with fantastic funny ears
Easily hear their pitiful prey underground
Trying desperately to suppress movement.
Mothering, made easier by her fiercely
Protective mate, is firmly focused.
These busy den dwellers sleep outside
Possibly to marvel at the bright starry sky.
No, you say?
Never underestimate the power of awe
In all critters great and small.

Iguanas leave their dens, not wanting to
Hide from the dazzling scorching sun.
They, unlike most, enjoy basking in it.
When chilly, they scurry into their burrows
Hibernating like a bear.
Their hatchlings fend for themselves
With no need of mom's attention.
Being fearless climbers, they will risk
A fall to reach buds, leaves or the fruit
Of a fan shaped Doum Palm.
These solitary "baby dinosaurs" do not
Notice nature's indifference and live a
Simple desert life with few demands.

You'd think the Desert Tortoise would
Enjoy days on end in the hot sun.
They, instead, laze under rocks or shrubs
With a preference for their desert "cave,"
Along with others like the Roadrunner
(sacred to indigenous people),
Gila Monster (venomous lizard) and
Burrowing Owl (who do little burrowing of
their own), they all, too, call the tortoise's
Home theirs!
Yet turtles being who they are, don't raise
A fuss, and welcome them as they must,
Excavating another if needed…
Going along to get along….

The name Javelina sounds like a dainty
Little butterfly, but can give a fright when
Faced with this small wild boar-like
Creature weighing in at 45 pounds.
With protruding sharp teeth, these
Herbivores are not interested in you,
But prefer tender green vegetation.
Living in large families, these intelligent
Peccaries can make affectionate pets
On the farms of those who appreciate
Their adorable attentive ways.
When attacked, however, these
2 foot dynamos can fend off cougars,
Coyotes, bobcats and others who
Quickly learn to back off, for now.
These gregarious "giants" would rather be
Buddies with the Desert Stones, who
Never cause trouble and speak only truth.

Snakes and scorpions
Bats and woodpeckers
Meerkats and Sand Cats
Gazelles and rats
Hyenas and toads
Salamanders and beetles
Locusts and Silver ants
Wrens and vultures
Hawks, spiders and jackrabbits.
You get the picture-
Barren rocky soil is far from boring.
This convention of all
Add to the desert's intrinsic beauty.

A biologically rich habitat is what the
Pearly Starry Nights and
Sparkling White Stones call HOME.

Animal Kingdom

By Jane A Lenzen

Human animals enjoy comparisons
Who has the largest house
The brightest kid
The prettiest pet
The finest clothes
The most "likes"
The biggest diamond
The best seat in the house.

Non human animals gain joy from
A rollick in the woods
Building a nest
Digging in dirt or snow
Stretching in the sun
Hanging with the herd
Romantic strutting
Grooming their baby

What makes any animal superior?
Nothing.....
Neither color nor size
Wealth or education
Muscular strength
Elegance or beauty
Intelligence or personality
Athletic endeavors

All animals are similar
We scurry around with intent
Protect our helpless young
War with our enemies
Become jealous over whatever
Believe in a supreme being
Build things
Create artwork
Work hard or have fun
Ponder situations, analyze thoughts
Grieve
Feast on each other
Dream
Talk, sing, laugh, cry, smile and play
Cultivate friendships and trust
Tease others
Plan

Is the human animal superior to others?
We tend to think so and use names of
animals in a demeaning way, such as "bird
brain" or "monkey mind." In a century we'll
realize how naïve this was.

To think this idea to be true is similar
to giving an American IQ exam to an
untouched civilization of tribal peoples,
then labeling them dumb or stupid because
they didn't pass the test.

We're all within the same Kingdom:
ANIMALIA

Undefined

By Jane A Lenzen

We cannot be defined by
What confines us.
Unlike a leopard's spots, we can change
As the flapping of a bird's wings
Helps to soar higher without restraint.

Either people mosey through life
Without the first thought of
Where it's headed,
Or study it until days take shape and form
A likelihood of meaning and purpose.
Neither is the right or wrong path.

Rising tension, however,
Exposes unconsciousness.
Not understanding what's deep inside
Stifles expression.
Once we realize that we can accept
Our weaknesses without defining them,
The soul becomes freer to be real.

Conformity stabs the heart of authenticity.
Judgements make sad statements
About those who stepped out of the box
To be who they were meant to be.
Radical spirits enable diverse thoughts
With a mental dynamic that allows
Fairness without casting pain or
Blame on other beings.

Renounce anything that does not
Resonate with the depth of your being.
When done consistently people around
You need not feel the need to be defined.
To fearlessly launch into your inner space
Knowing that it benefits both you and
The universe is the only way to live a life
Of genuine service to the world in an
Undefined manner that just feels right.

Habitats
By Jane A Lenzen

The loggers move in, indiscriminately slashing trees and brush,
all vegetation in its path.
They are only doing their jobs, you say. Yet they choose not to witness the startled
woodpeckers quickly taking flight while a mother tries, in vain, to save her nest of babies
eager to fledge.

The very foundations of their world shaken to its core.

The old oaks, long leaf pines, hickorys, American chestnuts, lichens, redwoods, yews,
buttonwoods, cypress, deer moss, dog fennel, and swamp sunflowers, just to name a
few, succumb to the perilous instability over time with few surviving the onslaughts
perpetuated by man.

Native gopher tortoises, panthers, whooping cranes, groundhogs, bees, toads,
grasshoppers, bear, wild turkey, coyotes, tiny soil critters, arthropods and invertebrates
that no one notices..... tenacious stray cats no one wants.
Where to go after evacuation?

Once settled in a new section of the world, will their sense of security be curtailed again
by a wealthy bored real estate tycoon with nothing better to do?

Eventually we see these critters in our own neighborhoods, seeking food and shelter in
the very place they once lived.

Now the frightening noises grow louder and vibrations never heard or felt before creep in
closer and closer. Should I stay or should I go? The rabbits freeze with fear.
Turtles can't leave as quickly as the snakes.
Many destroyed under the weight of the machinery.
Animal and plant culture ruined.

Days and days on end of land annihilation all appears so benign,
The fragmentation so innocent.
A few less trees, less oxygen, so what!
This soil, a longtime sustenance for many, becomes a money pit for others.

Machinery keep coming in
one after another. Loud, irritating screeches against the disappearing elegant landscape.

"What are they doing to our homes where we've lived for centuries? What could be more important than this land that we intuitively understand and nourish? We live in harmony and respect the ancient balance of the natural world. The peace we have always known in this territory, destroyed in just a few weeks by a tsunami of metal. How can this be? What is more important than this glorious part of our innate circular system of life?"

The bulldozing is done and the dependable, delightful noisy nighttime hum of crickets is eerily silenced among half drunk plastic bottles of water.

Earth shattering destruction makes way for another unnecessary acquisition for humans, who have a plethora of choices on where to spend their money or years.

No worries. An earth full of spectacular forests yet to be flattened. God, after all, gave it to man to do with what he wants, right?

Human created displacements or extinctions of animals, plants and tiny organisms all for shopping centers, office buildings, cattle, chicken and hog raising, parking lots, coal mining, condos, houses, amusement parks, and even zoos, an oxymoron. You get the point.......paving paradise to put up a parking lot...thanks Joni, but few took heed.....
stood silent like in Silent Spring.
In what way is this so difficult to understand?

Why the rush to slash and burn native lands when we know what we know? How can these creatures compete with man's insatiable desire for bigger and more?

What happened to failed conservation attempts of threatened plants and animals, like the gregarious Passenger Pigeons who obscured blue skies during flight?
Where is the stunning snow white headed Labrador Duck, or the St. Helena olive tree, an ecological beauty?
Thousands have been decimated, many of which man has never seen.
What magical ocean creatures have lived and died, due to man's pollution, without being noticed? No matter.
Coral reefs can be replaced.

Where is human sympathy for other creatures we deem unimportant? Instincts seem deadened to this zero-sum reality.

Man, over a short time, has singlehandedly upset Biodiversity.

Research proves that oblivious humans cause a decline in their own wellbeing but we can't seem to help ourselves.....this lack of awareness concerning our interdependence is so obvious to some but not to most.

The nighttime hum of critters is eerily silenced over and over again and, at some point, we might join them unless we subdue our own ignorant inclinations.

Whatsoever Proverbs

By Jane A Lenzen

Whatsoever encircles, be still
Whatsoever is wise, cling tightly
Whatsoever shouts, vibrate slower
Whatsoever supports, lean into
Whatsoever demands, keep boundaries
Whatsoever leads, look before following
Whatsoever ameliorates, keep building
Whatsoever penetrates, study & discern
Whatsoever causes doubt, rethink it
Whatsoever traverses, creates footsteps
Whatsoever feels unattainable, be patient
Whatsoever illuminates, add to the light
Whatsoever seems pejorative, don't judge
Whatsoever saddens, look up
Whatsoever emerges, do not resist
Whatsoever hardens, can bend
Whatsoever tempts, strengthens you
Whatsoever promotes tears, subdues
Whatsoever shifts, trains the brain
Whatsoever is funny, changes the face
Whatsoever convicts, others may scorn
Whatsoever helps them, may hinder you
Whatsoever dwells within, keep purified
Whatsoever is resilient, hold on
Whatsoever disciplines, creates habits
Whatsoever detects spirit, takes root
Whatsoever dignifies, maintains growth
Whatsoever you mock, look in the mirror
Whatsoever impedes, go around
Whatsoever you utter, be deliberate
Whatsoever shouldn't be, is
Whatsoever promotes curiosity, teaches
Whatsoever dances, laughs

Reflections

By Jane A Lenzen

A teenager throughout the '60's
Experiences like no other
A common thread wove its way into
the hearts and naive minds of us all.
Such promise....

Love, inequalities and war imprinted on
Brains of blank sheets.
A Rolling Stone crashed the psyche,
piercing young souls with
grandiose and conflicting messages.

Music, marches and faith saved us all
Allowing expressions to expand.
Zippered lips slowly opened to
voices that couldn't be quelled.

We continuously danced and danced
To varied rhythms that no other
Generation could follow-
The steps were distinct, novel
The notes too intense,
all immersed within a fiery fury
of innocence…
eventually lost.

As an arrow released from its bow
There was no stopping us.
Until
The Passage of Time

Recognizing the endless cycles -
A sequence of events that
Build upon each other….
We realize that our boomer generation
was no more unique or special
than any other era.

Destination
By Jane Alise Lenzen

When prophets give testimony
To the grand scheme of things
The past present and future
Of where we will eventually be.

Take heed of the words
Look in the rear view mirror
Observe where you came from,
Reorient when possible, then TAKE FLIGHT!

Listen to the powerful way
That wisdom leads
Without struggle or force,
Evolving into understanding.

The Hand that leads you to
A familiar place that comforts,
One that you once knew well
But got off track.

Open your eyes and look around.
Steadfast and determined,
Your journey is renewed.
All hesitation has ceased.

You are home once again.

Thought Less

By Jane A Lenzen

Situations seen through a particular lens
Define identity through tangible moments,
Ontological ideas with grand illusions.

Inner woundings function secretly
Navigating through a private headspace
With residual effects unknown.

Tough questions with few answers
On the intricacies of unspoken trauma;
Where to turn outside your mind.

The embattled brain looks away
Having dealt with it bravely, yet
Dwelling on the details
Seems an exercise in futility,
Like feet sinking deeper in the sand.

This intenseness must incorporate
Into the ultimate aim of correlating
It all into a broader scope,
Keeping a simple perspective in view.

A moment and eternity are the same,
An emblematic relationship
Requiring no explanation.
If topsy turvy recollections bring you
To your knees, dig a hole in the sand
And bury them. Then arise a lighter
More Thought Less person, rid of
Memories that cause sorrow.

The imagination, more real than reality,
Can bring joy to the fore.
Life's journey finds expression in the vast
Depository of ideas and creations which
Develop without force and coercion,
Allowing spontaneous sparks to sizzle.

"Elan vital" where past and present meet,
Finally becoming friends.
Coherence and conscience converge
Within a multiplicity of thoughts…
Eventually finding peace within
Thought Less Ness.

Pink No Better Than Gray

By Jane A Lenzen

No one is less equal than the next.
We harbor iron clad ideas of
What defines equality.
Many feel superior. Why?

Money, power, prestige
Unevenly distributed.
Success matters not
When others are under foot.

Geo politics down to small neighborhoods
View interconnectedness from space,
Seeing components of similarities.
Each story told, stirs and enlightens.

Tight integration is key
To falling in love with each other.
Wonderfully diverse groups
Comprise richness unrivaled.

Equality negates hubris while
Accepting others' differences.
Cultures are inter-reciprocal and
Rearrange ideas about the other.

Someone sees weeds in the lawn
While another, garden delights;
One who views another human less than,
Must view himself superior, similar to a
Rose verses a dandelion…
The core essence is all the same
Similar to snow verses rain
Or pink verses gray.

So one with surplus helps another
Avoid precipitous events.
Expanded ideas always sustain.
Inclusion spreads like a beautiful breeze.
But characterizing identities negatively
Tear down unifying principals.

One who dwells in a hut could teach
Great lessons to another in a mansion.
Immersion into others' backgrounds
Discovers new ways, how each views
This world of which we all partake.
Every one gains, no one loses.

We all stare at stars and sunrises
At different times and locales.
From a mountaintop or a desert
Humans view the moon's craters and
Highlands with the same almost spherical
Looking eyes. If blind, they can listen to
a Description which tickles the brain's
Imagination no matter who the listener is.

Outer appearances may be unique, but
Life essentials much the same.
Skin hues may differ, yet once dead
Skeletons are pretty indistinguishable.

53

Sappho

By Jane A Lenzen

Breaking barriers, this "sapphire" poet
Discerning, poised, with laughing eyes
Broke through with nimble self expression
Where no woman had ever gone before.

Like a small asteroid, Sappho orbited into
Greek literature as the 10th muse,
Which most likely amused her
Delicate sensibilities as absurd!

Her paeans displayed clear depth
Using great sublimity of words,
Yet piercing with extreme emotion.
Sparrows, doves, swans, even roses
Would take heed of Sappho supplications
Making sure Aphrodite heard her cries.

Kerkylas of Andros would have adored
Sappho if he only knew of her.
Her unrequited love for Phaon
Lead to a leap off Leucadian cliffs?
These lurid tales would cause Sappho to
Wish she'd written about such drama!

Her family, exiled, evoked much emotion
Which was alleviated by her support of
Siblings' unfulfilled aristocratic dreams.
Morale was heightened by Sappho's
Spontaneous and steadfast devotion.

The contrast of love of family with
Love sickness for another person
Shattered the very soul of Sappho,
Who, with great similar longing,
Could not grasp the highest most
Beautiful red blushing apple on a tree.
Both beyond reach…created unsatiated
Desire and great hunger.

Since "gods do what they like,
And call down hurricanes with a whisper,"
Sappho begs for relief once more.
Where else can she turn to rid the heart
Of such primal aching?
Feeling like an outlaw in her own body,
Sappho felt distress by her inability to
Overcome primal unsated urges.
The sun's rays warming her sensual
Nature will, for the moment, suffice.

Sappho's reverie comes to the fore…
Passions dance in holy places
Where the bride and groom flow
With the sweet sound of the flute
Against the clanging of cymbals.
The scents of cassia, myrrh and
Frankincense rise to the heavens
Mingled with maidens and men singing,
Women wailing, knowing virginity
Is soon to be painfully taken.

Bold ventures into matters of the heart
As a strong wind assaults an oak tree,
Has her reader staring at the mirror
While nodding, "Yes, I know of her pain."
While she dealt with severed bits of
Her being, she also knew that deep
Down inside, things will surely get better.
Are these hopes due to maturity or just
Wishful thinking from a naive woman?
Irregardless, singing her poetic lines with
A Lilting Lyre alongside a large cup of
Wine will promote much defiant dancing,
Forgetting all imagined or real troubles
And internal resistance.

So sweet Sappho, your lament that
No one would remember you
After your last dying breath,
Proved to be false in the end and
Since 615 BC you are still admired
For such brave thoughts in a draconian
Time when few spoke of such things.

Zeus, honoring your prayers, made sure
Your Name, with
Sapphic meter, endured, and your
Lips were never stricken to silence.
Aphrodite and Eros be praised!

POETRY and PROSE

By Jane A Lenzen

A Rhapsody where words tickle the mind
An idea blossoms without effort
The heart and mind may ache, giggle or
soar with each idea expressed.

Every word must earn its keep:

Thundering surf
Patiently disembark
Existential godliness
Haunting recollections
Aesthetic philosophy
Eager conclusions
Narcotic moments
Banal pleasantries

What feelings do these word pairs evoke?
Most likely, a different meaning to each
pair of ears.

How to finish the lines
What fits, what is discarded?
Provocative questions
With answers asking more.
Poets, like natural events,
Succumb easily to atmospheric tones.
Yet words will continuously flow
Like wind patterns around the globe.

Sometimes the poem has a mind of its
Own and the poet must respect this.
So go ahead and take it to its occasional
Illogical conclusion because someone
Out there will possibly benefit from it.

Like a rollercoaster bending into twilight
Be content with its ups and downs
Soaring to an eventual getting off point.
When it speaks an idea fervently, listen.
Allow it to move into the sunset, as it will
Rise again tomorrow
To speak words of endless creativity.
Phraseology? Who cares?!

Cognitive dissonance reigns
Heightening rather obscure notions.
Nurturing each phrase like a
Child cradling a beloved pet.

Then finally, with a tiny feeling of triumph
The poem is at last complete.

Home or Far Afield

By Jane A Lenzen

Some seldom or never stray from home
The yearnings never tickled the mind
Maybe fear of flying or traveling to
Unknown territories is unsettling,
Routines severely disrupted.

A cloistered existence may make for a
Placid more peaceful life.
There's little variety to local outings
Every inch of area familiar, including
Faces at the grocer or doctor's office.

The explorer craves the adventure
Yet unprepared for whatever challenges
Suddenly strike...Like when
Magellan stepped into tribal warfare,
A tourist could be
Caught in cartel crossfire in Mexico.

Extensive travelers don't give it a thought.
Fear is drowned by a swim in the sea,
Swallowed by tastes of Yoshoku in Japan.
Exploration is its own reward.
Traversing unknown parts of the world
Gives one new perspectives
Just unique enough to fascinate:

Elephants roaming free or Giant Pandas
at play. Won't see that in your backyard.
A tropical deciduous Forest Fantasy or a
Trip to an Istanbul Spice Bazaar,
Iguazu Falls in South America can take
one's breath away
A "Rocky Mountain High" in the Andes

How about a dive into the magnificent
Mediterranean Sea or a ride on a camel
around the Great Pyramids of Giza
A solemn prayer at the Western Wall
The colossal Colosseum in Rome
New Zealand coastlines or
Iceland fjords will exhilerate
as would thousands more options.

Traversing unknown parts of our world is
exciting, yet for the less inclined, a nice
walk in a local park with your dog will do.
What a uniquely keen observer notices
can be just as spectacular as
any exotic in another country.

Cultivate a new appreciation for your own
home town, by taking advantage of

-Local talent at the playhouse
-Libraries, museums, historic districts
-Neighborhood specialty shops
-International cuisines
-Beautiful places of worship
-Rivers, streams, lakes or waterfalls
-Meadows, mountains or oceans
-Caves, canyons, monuments, gardens
-Free roaming wild animal parks

No packing, long drives or flying...
Elegant enjoyment at your fingertips
Always ready to please.

BELIEF

By Jane A Lenzen

Adherence to a belief....
Premonitions ignored....
Rigid rules followed.
Many straining to understand why
Fervent supplications go unanswered.

Inquisitors who keep vigil
In order to inherit the Kingdom,
Ignore the sin of gluttony while
Maintaining the word of God,
Who cringes at man's vain prayers.

Belief systems, like a flickering candle,
Burn bright for awhile, then may be
Reduced to smoke from a simple breeze.
Once relit, the wax clumps from a fire
Intent on burning the passion of faith.

The choir of angels rebel against
Coerced conversions
Where religious fervor is soon to be like
Ice on tree limbs, which melt when
The sun glares and wind changes course.
This entices the eager heavenly
Host to shower love on confused minds
While giving gentle nudges toward simple
Understandings and clarity.

No supervision need be required
Of truly devout petitioners.
Through focused cloistered minds
Some are disciplined seekers
Of inner wisdom vs fleeting fancy.
In time, resolute minds discriminate, and
The aspirant finds his personal conviction,
Causing ethereal beings to rejoice
While the Creator
Simply smiles.

Evolution

By Jane A Lenzen

When viewing things as a catastrophe
Make a quick alteration and see it as
A simple inconsequential irritation.
Then like a miracle
It may dissolve.

Hours can be spent wishing
The moments were different
A point in time that is truly sweet
Intruded upon us by
Troubling thoughts.

Concern over a future event that
So seldom occurs-
Anxiety over minute details
Add to imaginary conundrums,
Lumbering ahead with dread.

When thoughts quickly mushroom
Creating self inflicted havoc
Where none surrounds us,
We must dream a story of
Ideas that segue to a relative truth:
The exquisite rawness of our interior
Is speaking false imagined narratives!

An Evolutionary Musing might go
like this......

No fodder for fiction here
Since an erudite knows
The Difference between
Words in the head and reality.

What is their secret?

They compare both sides with fairness
Viewing content of experience lightly,
especially when emotional winds
shift to the negative.
Innate genius always directs cells
toward Wisdom, eternally present.

Then, like a gift, performance receives
Thunderous applause from all atoms
Residing in every cell of the body-
Healing occurs without trying-
The moment now awakens
An underlying credulity
Of what is present

And all is well
....

Time

By Jane A Lenzen

Time, whether it exists or not
Seems to tether us regardless.
When effort is put into fruitless action
We say it's wasted.
If something's accomplished, we rejoice
And satisfaction seeps in.
We say "time flies" when having fun.

Time is not cumulative nor curious
It cares little if you fritter it away
And laughs when you frantically try
Catching up, with little success;
Like being late to a meeting causing a
Menacing mental roar… to RUSH!!

Time doesn't mind being ignored
Actually, it rather enjoys it.
When lost in the present moment,
Time flourishes into eternity.

Because time knows that humans
Are excellent at futuring and pasting
It creates provocative moments like wind
In a hurricane, causing aggrieved states
In order to PAY ATTENTION!

Many moons come and go
Vineyards are planted and we work
And wait until, finally, grapes are ripe
Crushed and strained.
Once bottled, years must accrue.
Patience eventually pays off
With the first delightful sip.

Then what do we do in the meantime?
Time still passes while we wait-
So we focus on other important matters.
Some pleasurable, some not.

Once calm is reclaimed, however,
One, at last, learns that
Racing, rushing, coming and going
Has little to do with spending time wisely
Yet time can't be spent, right?
So, you might as well take it easy.
Then and only then does the concept
Of time melt away into contentment
And the lungs can finally enjoy a very
Long….deep…breath. Aahh…..

Holiness

By Jane A Lenzen

Who among us is truly holy?
Someone who can reign in impulses?
Has more compassion than most?
Who has mastered the raging ego?

Angry words never leave their lips
No situation creates inner calamity
Safety is of little importance
The heart matches up with actions

Their is no deceit or coverup
A sanctuary lives within
Motives do not exist
It can be no other way

They refuse to be followed
As leadership does not denote character
They decline being put on a pedestal
To be worshipped is ridiculous

Their knowledge impossible to explain
Pretense is nonexistent
Unaware of their perfection
They blissfully go about their business

Adulation is laughable
Complements unnecessary
Since no effort was made
To do anything extraordinary

Words and actions are unobtrusive
Since they know their intentions may be
Misinterpreted by a morally numb world,
Irregardless, achievements are common

Righteousness repels any adulation
No need to obtain greatness
Their every thought and deed is pure
With nothing expected in return

They never feel used or cheated
It is over when it was over
Food, water and shelter is plenty
Butterflies and birds always bring joy

Things are as they are
They do not resist suffering
Equanimity in all things
Forcing ideas on others, fruitless

Humility never fails them
Like nature, everything at its own pace
Though pettiness thrives everywhere
This silliness has no effect

Intentions are always honorable
Sentiments are not exalted
Spiritual battles seldom lost
As the essence within is unchanging

Do As I Please

By Jane A Lenzen

The world is my oyster,
Inspiring me to take what I deserve.
Humans must multiply to
Maintain economic strength.
Mother Earth can make room…
Wide open spaces are a bore.

Children can pretty much take care
Of themselves just like I did.
No real need for much oversight as
Day care and older siblings can help.
I grew up poor and we were on our own
Very young and did OK.
So kids do not interfere with my
Ambitions and ignoring irritating cries
Makes them stronger. Diapering can wait.
Better yet, a swift back hand
Can shut them up. I often wonder
Just like my mom,
Why I had them in the first place.

I can ignore my aches and pains as
They're nothing to crow about since
My medications do the trick.
If I work extremely hard I will remain
Competitive and gain more wealth.
Big returns are right around the corner.
No welfare checks for me.

I can easily ignore the peculiar notion
That pollution is some huge problem.
Let big tech find the solutions for all
This excess garbage.
My cough is not really a major issue,
The air seems pure enough to me.
There are bigger causes for concern,
Like inflation and gas prices neither of
Which will force me to tighten my belt as I
Worked hard for my stuff and
Want to show it off before I grow old.

The water ways are tainted you say.
Oh, all these provocative narratives-
They look fine to me.
My boat glides through easily….
Kill a Manatee? They are too slow and
Must learn to get out of the way.
My fishing excursion (without the whiners)
Produced a King Mackerel for dinner.
Did not taste a bit of mercury.

The brown haze has always been here.
Did it look that different 100 years ago?
I don't think so…Again, fear-mongering.
Every generation deals with something.
I enjoy my life and am poised for success.
My priorities are in order.

Don't misunderstand me,
I care about my family and our planet
It's just that these haughty people
Are overreacting, saying our grandkids
Will have to deal with it. Blah, blah, blah
Well, I'm going to live my life the same as
My friends and neighbors do and
Enjoy what the world has to offer,
Only better.

Fountain of Elders

By Jane A Lenzen

The quest for youth,
Yearning to postpone
Biological processes

Enthralled with memories,
Evading the present
Physiological changes

Circulating impulses
Move around the mind,
Tempting, yet
Impossible to fulfill

Was 16 really so sweet?
The time clock asks,
Would you relive your youth?
Are these eloquent visions reliable?

When thinking of my dad and dogs
A comfort level arises knowing that
Each dealt with passing years
Tenaciously yet with tenderness.
Admired older siblings pave the way for
Younger ones who can glean much

Daunting decades may compromise
Physical properties but
Manipulation of ego is gladly muted.
We are candid and guileless
Knowing our overall strengths without
The lure of ads promoting longevity pills!

The Fountain of Elders
Has arrived in full force,
With a reservoir of wise words
Touching all who yearn for advise
Listen and learn, youngsters
Your day will soon come

Welcoming the Self

By Jane A Lenzen

Other focused, years on end
Seeing needs, then jumping in
Desperate pleas everywhere
We can help, yep, we'll be there.

Why the suffering, why the pain
Can we assure them of some gain?
Hand up, hand out, doesn't matter
Anything to calm the clatter.

Running here, racing there
With goals to always make things fair
Asians helping African Americans
Blacks serving Native Americans
Whites giving Hispanics a hand
Latinos helping Mexicans to stand.
People embracing other people
To stand erect like a steeple.

Yet some years later, looking back
Feeling like we got off track
Who were we in the midst of this
Always racing towards an abyss.

Did we help or did we squander
Could our years have been much fonder
No, not really, because compassion
Will always be within our fashion.

Doing quietly without fuss
Gentle aid without the lust
For accolades or recognition,
Does not feed the inner condition.

The biggest difference is now the pace
We no longer feel we're in a race.
When the need presents itself
We can safely put it on the shelf.

Until our inner selves are fed and
Yielding to the need for bed
Observing all the others' wants
We now no longer feel the taunts.

We've welcomed us into the realm
With a new position at the helm.
Navigating fully in the moment
Not allowing guilt to foment.

Thank you, selves, for realizing
Compassion can be tantalizing
Look within to see what's there, and
If not able, we will declare....

"I cannot concede to this agenda
Quiet spirit is now my mantra
Finally time to feed my soul
The solitude has made me whole."

Millions out there understand
That one who's spent cannot stand
We now set boundaries to get restored
First, to feed our inner core.

The pressure's off and we are steady
Fully prepared now and on the ready
Look around, see saints among us
As bright beacons on silver canvas.

Intention BEHIND Death

By Jane A Lenzen.

Connection to everything that exists,
Certain that some entity beyond
Our capacity to know, lives on. Yet,
Cannot demand it to be a certain way.

Biblical texts studied for a lifetime
History memorized and challenged.
Religions teach outer bounds and hope,
Genuine rules of life that may work.

Delayed Gratification, Psychological
Tenacity doesn't deprive us of joy.
Mature minds find delight in little things.
Is death the final moral perfection?

Still, after our demise, little is known
Other than stories of streets of gold,
A paradisiacal Gan Eden or
Rustic images yearning for
A rainbow leading to perfection.

If we could open Venetian blinds
Take a peek into the world to come
And witness laughter vs longings
What vast changes would we make?

Having witnessed your future existence
Would it make these allotted days better?
If we knew that death was the start of
Eternity.....What does that look like...
This Foreshadow of Foreverness.

Infinity, a word not adequately defined.
What to do each day without end
Relationships permanently protected
No need to ever hurry.....

If death, however, is being dead forever
The urgency of doing grows strong
With awe and wonder being sacrificed
To a wildly escalating drumbeat.

With an interest in how things began
Many ponder the Great Life Force....
The caveman looked up to the heavens
Was he so different from us?

Maybe death, which
Releases trapped tension,
Unburdened by the body,
Floats on stardust particles
Giving counsel to loved ones through a
Gentle whisper

All part of a celestial voice
Tenderly proclaiming

Peace at Last

Contrasts & Hidden Meanings

By Jane A Lenzen

Examine each line
Whatever comes to mind
Speak aloud to hear what you find!

Feathers-Flowers, climb to the towers
Taste-Swallow, no longer hollow
Good-Bad, smile, be glad
Black-White, a beacon in the night
Hot-Cold, sensations too bold
Elated-Sad, choice to be had
Far-Near, witness a tear
Move-Still, atop a great hill
North-South, quiet the mouth
Left-Right, neither has might
Awake-Asleep, you can go deep
Animal-Plant, neither say can't
Expose-Cover, and love one another
Light-Dark, a walk in the park
Open-Closed, neither exposed
Nice-Mean, easily seen
In-Out, neither can tout
Tiger-Lily, both think we're silly
Powerful-Weak, forces to seek
Fake-Real, neither conceal
Order-Chaos, gone with a toss
Enemy-Friend, discern and attend
Sink-Buoyant, may be clairvoyant
Religious-Secular, both too particular
Hidden-Revealed, better left sealed
Cynical-Naive, avoid your pet peeve
Heaven-Earth, both can give birth
Wide-Narrow, straight as an arrow

Truth-Lie, can too easily tie
Stingy-Generous, no need to be timorous
Snow-Fire, make you jump higher
Horizontal-Vertical, both very practical
Hungry-Full, a motivational tool
Old-New, as the sweet morning dew

Transcendent God

By Jane A Lenzen

God in all, independent, yet spanning
Creation like a vascularized network
Supplying life-giving sustenance-
Everything necessary to thrive.
This Higher Realm's vast reach
Is found everywhere
Seen and unseen

The Abrahamic God of the universe in
Union with holy prophets and teachers
Moses, Deborah, Job, Elijah, Elisha, Isaiah,
Ezekiel, Jeremiah, Josiah, Maimonides,
Jesus, John, Joan, Teresa, Fox, Gandhi, King,
Mandela, Graham and
Millions of other wise women and men
Whose steadfast faith and valor was
Guided from above and within,
Embodying concepts of universal
Principles implanted into all beings
From the womb

This same Supreme Being known by
Zoroastrians, Baha'i's, Buddhists, Laozi,
Confucius, Druze, Hindus, Muslims, Jainists,
Sikh's, Native Americans - all
Abide by the call of the
Great Spirit who calms
Evil inclinations and warrior whims within

Kindness courted, hatred held at bay
In all seekers of spirit;
Sincere adherents, transcending dogma
Do not take Faith lightly

A knowing is implanted in us from Birth...
Dampened by the world over time -
Rediscovering what is
Already present is key

No need to see to believe
Instead, believe to see...
The soul always knows

To breathe is to grok God
The air becomes part of you
And you part of the air.
One feeds the other who in turn
Nourishes the very nature of being

We can study, memorize, have sincere
Devotion to religion
Yet none is necessary if we look
At our surroundings as a child,
Reigniting the wonder-
Witnessing the miracle in
Blades of grass

Transcendent God found in all,
No one having exclusivity on Truth-
Innately Imprinted on our brains.
Various religions and philosophies speak
Mysteries into hearts, yet
We can intuit God without words,
Speak to Supreme Being any time
Anywhere

The simplicity of a relationship with Diety
Is profound…
The mainstay and sustenance of life.
Talk to God with receptive reverence
Every thought, word and deed
Connected to Source always
Provides peace within

Spirit is eternal and all moral codes
Derive from it naturally.
Celestial noble messages eagerly
Heard by receptive ears

Aligned with holiness
You become as a tree
Sustained by living waters,
Sturdy and Strong forevermore

God accepts our meager
Understandings when coming from a pure
Heart whose goal is to
Walk the path of passion, by having a
Devotion to Goodness
Knowing that our Vast and Virtuous
Everlasting Creator holds all universes in
The Bosom of Being,
We relinquish total control

Taking our head out of the clouds
We notice the underlying Unity within,
The sanctity of
Ruach rising and falling
Satisfying longings of the soul

Ultimate Reality is hidden in one
Grand Holistic principle where we
Witness Divine presence in:

the curiosity of a child
caterpillar to butterfly
kindness of strangers
a deep yawn
laugh of a old man
a pelican dive
graveside wreaths
first summer watermelon
compassion for unlovables
ants working in unison
smell of rain
weaving of a spider
ancient biblical texts
lilting sea cucumbers

Be still and know that "I AM God"
Who transcends all thought and words

Listen and look carefully-
A Mockingbird, singing a sacred song.
This glorious gift outside your window
Noticed for the very first time

Observation requires so little of us
Walk outside and listen with intent

The Mockingbird begins to vigorously
Sing its heart out
Because her exalted tune is heard
And appreciated by you
For the very first time

A simple transcendent moment with God

Cognitive Shifts

By Jane A Lenzen

Chaos washes over us
insufferable at times
Yet we plunge onward.
Perfection need not exist
Flexibility in all things
like a leaf zigzagging down a river
Finding comfort within
Quirkiness

Discomfort arises that becomes
Unbearable…the malady worsening
By the moment until a Shift takes place.
Angels direct a mental labyrinth
Beaming light into a stagnant mind.
Calm in the midst of misery with
Variations and fluctuations all
Within our sacred cerebral space
Giving brilliance to extravagant
Randomness and geospatial
Complexity

Prolific wisdom wasted on those
Whose ears temporarily don't hear;
Inability to comprehend expressions
Simply stated by others. Yet, these
Misunderstood commonalities may give
Rise to a Eureka Moment where
Spontaneous Insight convicts and
A new clue into the conversation
Is suddenly realized and cultivated.
An open bond ensues coupled with
A new sense of ease with each other.
Transcendence

We listen to a Billy Joel song over and
Over, sing the fun lyrics enthusiastically
Enjoy the excitement of a concert
Yet may not hear the poetry behind
Words written by contemplative artists.
Once we sit quietly digesting the lines
Of intent behind heartfelt words, we
Perceive meaning and wisdom within
Creativity and a little segment of our
Soul Soars

Stewing on a problem or hurt
We lash out or sulk to prove a point.
They are wrong-we are right
How do they not see this?
Yet once we take some time as in
Making a loaf of bread from scratch,
The kneading of dough softens us.
Allowing it to rise TWICE provides
Time to ponder on events that now
Appear laughable.
We hug our "offender" and say
"I am sorry. This is not of any import."
Reviewing the incident with
Honest eyes, both sides are now
Clearly Visible

Various examples of simple incongruity
Until a Cognitive Shift takes place
Imposing strong intrinsic intuition -
Knowing these encounters are versions
of what has come before in various
Evolutionary Situations

We soon realize events become quite
Manageable knowing confusion won't
Cling to us no matter the circumstances.
Thoughts stay steady-We listen more
Intently to ourselves and others
Our resolve to respect does not falter
As a shift to understanding is
Continually Renewed

Wolf and Lamb Unified

By Jane A Lenzen

Insinuations can have consequences
Implications may be fact or not
What is truth to some is false to another
A solicited summation is of import
To whom and for what purpose?

Ultimate Reality, like prayer, needs no
Sentences finished, as Divinity Dazzles &
Confers with no validation required.
It explodes and contracts with irrevocable
Splendor without involvement with
Right or wrong, ally or foe.

Theological arguments stifle the soul,
Separating each other with
The need to be right.
Creeds and dogma divide those with
Differing understandings.

Spirit moves mysteriously, yet with
Discipline, invulnerable to man's whims.
The Divine need not persuade, as all
Is obvious to even an infant in a crib,
Whose dependency on parents is as
Ours on the Spiritual Realm who created
The Cosmological Crib we live in.

When awakened to a simple knowing,
Displaying a dogmatic position wanes.
The Supreme is not vague. It has power to
pierce and expose vanity, yet pours out
Protection on its offspring similar to the
Ease of our tenderness toward our own.
What Is more dear or enduring than
Looking into the scintillating eyes of your
Newborn, where a dialogue begins.
The love of God for its creation is
Embedded in our psyche as well.

As a deer pants, longing to lap water, We
thirst for the knowledge of a
Gracious God who peels layers of Ignorance
from our seared souls
Soon to be quenched and healed.

The Sovereign reigns over all with a
Balcony seat to everything that exists.
It Sings a Song that those with a
Pitch of Purity can hear,
Swaying to and fro in cosmic rhythm
To a tune that seems out of step with
Most who are inclined towards ignorance.

To realign we must focus on
Equality, not strength.
Listening, not talking,
Observing, not interfering.

Supreme Instinct does not divide but is
Symbiotic at its core, validating others'
differences and similarities when expressed
with eloquent kindness,
similar to dialogue between child and pet.

The wolf will then dwell with the lamb
The leopard with the goat
A calf and young lion, all led by a child
Cows' and bears' offspring
Rest together peacefully knowing that
None are superior to the other.

The universe finally speaking with
One Voice in such a unified way
as it would soon be considered
a curious thing indeed to be
anything otherwise.

Rat in Rationale

By Jane A Lenzen

RATIONALE: the reason in your head for doing what you do

RATIONAL: reasonable and appropriate Ideas that make sense to you.

RATION: having a limit on particular items that must be kept in circulation for the greater good.

RATIO: a mathematical calculation of quantities that help us understand the rational rationale behind the ration.

RAT: a word used to describe a snitch or deceitful person.

-In reality, the furry kind is actually very smart, enjoyed as a lovable pet or for humans in need of emotional support.
-Rats are able to sniff out gunpowder and land mines, heroically saving human lives.
-A pack of rats is called a "Mischief"… Seems logical enough.
-They can accurately detect TB in humans and are presently in training to smell early stage cancer and CoVid infections.
-They form wonderful family bonds and live in a complex social environment with psychological traits similar to ours.
-Rats groom themselves and others within their pack and are cleaner than we think.

India dedicated a temple to Karni Mata, the rat goddess, where people dutifully mingle with and feed 1000's of rats as a sign of respect since these furry critters were reincarnated from their ancestors to eventually become holy or regular humans again. Other regions of India think of rats as a delicious delicacy.
To each his own.

The Chinese zodiac placed the rat in first place ahead of the strongest of animals, the ox, which make sense to rat fanciers who view them as fascinating friends.

In ancient Japan they put rice cakes outside for rats to enjoy in celebration of the New Year and in Rome they were seen as either good or bad omens, depending on their shade of coat.

So the RATIONALE for disliking these clever rodents is not entirely RATIONAL. Mankind would greatly prefer to RATION the rat population or better yet exterminate the rodent completely.

In truth, the RATIO of RATS to humans does not cause any serious problems for society at large especially if we can use them to our advantage. However, lab studies using millions of rats (that humans produce) do not equate or transfer to the human body or brain and often redundant research causes pain and suffering to these sentient beings with results seldom if ever translating to a beneficial understanding of the problem studied.

If one has taken up residence in your home, there are humane ways (traps) to manipulate a positive outcome for both parties. (See photo)

Or enlist the services of a rescued kitty who would enjoy a challenging chase with a mischievous rat.

Speak to Me

By Jane A Lenzen

Tell me the story again
I want to hear the details
Of what matters to you and your world.

I can mingle with your serenity
Find comfort with authenticity
Listen to your heart that's been ignored.

You're a poetic vision of freedom,
A Bud that Blossoms with no pretense,
A virtuous person who cares not of fame
Nor of convention that stifles.

You do not fit into a tidy society which
Values vengeance when it feels
Deprived of what it seemingly deserves.

We both know that man with inherent
Defects must become acquainted with
The power of steady transformation.

As a righteous person you are acutely
Aware that thought and action are tied
To an accounting within eternal memory.

You are disturbed and at a low point
A place most serious thinkers visit,
Then remedy through Divine Grace.

We are as threads woven into cloth
Soaked in your tears.
I am damp with sorrow knowing you
Feel abandoned by all.

So sing your way to my ears that hear,
I'll read the silence of your soul
Consider the cause of your joy and pain
To rekindle a sense of selfless stirrings,
Temporarily lost.

This common ground on which we stand
Hands raised toward Divine Intent
While diving deep to kindle the souls
Of two people now swimming in unison
Pride and competition forever muted.

My gift to you are eyes that light up
A natural token of appreciation
Witnessing your integrity and faith.
I see in you a wondrous spirit.

This is a momentous moment that speaks
Much louder than simple words.
An arrow that pierces the cortex
Connecting one human to another
Through the soul of someone who
Embraced what society missed.

The Cloud Reigns

By Jane A Lenzen

There was Helios, Ra, Surya, Mithra, Inti Sol Invictis
and others shining brightly to lead ancient navigators on journeys far and near.
Venturing to unknown territories by sea and land were practically unfeasible when lowly
clouds hid Helios and Asteria from travelers. The puffy canopy would soon part, allowing
the adventurous expedition to continue.

The sky god, Zeus, with terrifying thunderbolts, ruled over Iris, the rainbow, Zephyrs, the
West Wind and all who lived in the sky and land for that matter.

Selene, silvery goddess of the moon and Helios' sister, seldom had to compete with the
cloud, who hadn't attained godhood and given very little respect by the great and fearful
Zeus. This never bothered the dignified cloud, well aware of its great worth and inward
power.

Anemi, the wind god, or Auta, goddess of the breeze could easily move the clouds along,
possibly with the help of Atlas, but could never force them to disappear since clouds had a
Mind of their own!

Even when Isis and Osiris visited from their sacred shrines, the clouds did not bow or
show particular reverence, as one god was no better than another. Clouds received them
as equals knowing one day all would be treated as such when they eventually came to
compassionate power.

Clouds felt no need for a god to direct their path. Governing themselves, these Condensed
Vapor Masses thought little of showing up when desired the least -
But cared not, for they knew their worth.

They formed haphazardly and enjoyed
floating above the world, occasionally unraveling numerous Nephelae, the nymphs,
(including Smilax, fairest of all) who danced in their favorite
Cottony Cumulus,
until exhaustion set in
When suddenly…
At midnight's darkness, they jumped into
their favorite White Fluff, falling fast
asleep, trusting that dreams be sweet,
Until Pele of the mountains erupted,
Roaring with a powerful stormy voice
Piercing all with lessons of intent.

Then, with certainty, the devoted
clamoring Cloud shouted with a
benevolent yet shivering shudder,
"Dance and live under harsh rule no more.
Stop and listen to my wise instructions
and in return I will feed your hungry souls."
Then as promised,
Joy and mercy reigned throughout
Under the kind and generous
Illuminated Benevolent Cloud of the Sky.
Goodness flourished and all were saved.

So the Mighty Cloud astonished all
By overcoming the odds.
Exhausted, Zeus surprised many as he
Felt relieved to be hidden by Cloud Cover,
His reign coming to a delightful end,
With the constant need to defend his
Throne, now a memory.
Finally Zeus could relish some rest
Knowing that his family would be safe and
The thirsty universe would be
Forevermore nourished and satiated.

All accomplished with benevolence
And a peaceful pass of power.

Everyone cheered and bowed to Cloud,
who chose Pegasus as its helper,
Inspiring rain and cool springs to quench
Thirsty souls.

Peace now reigned throughout and

Fairness over force
Won the day.

Crow Alert to the Sounds of Silence

By Jane A Lenzen

Walking in a hurried pace with intentions in full gear
I hear a crow call from overhead,
A song that distance intensifies
from silence all around.
Slow down. Stop.

With eyes closed, I strain a bit to
Listen to the silence,
To hear the air move,
The falling autumn leaves, easily plucked loose from stems so dry.....1, 3, 20 and more

I open my eyes to view the rustling rain of colors, just loud enough to marvel at
its sweet music and soft rhythm.
This same gentle breeze, ushering each leaf to earth, tenderly brushes my face, caressing
my being to such an extent that
Time Stood Still for Eternity

I was ONE with infinity through this wind,
connecting me with a natural
breathing essence of all that is.
Not seen by the eye, but experienced through
the simple call of a crow
and a gentle autumn wind.

Certainty in Ambiguity

By Jane A Lenzen

Sometimes we just don't know
And will never know
The answers to so many questions.

Biblical texts taken out of context
May satisfy certain yearnings for
Concrete conclusions.

Perceptual processes can paint
A narrow picture of truth
Where we manipulate words "to fit."

Our political biases are clung to when
An open-ended idea pops up,
Causing discomfort or even rage.

Is there a personality variable where
There is little interest in another's
Theory or innovative discussion?

Clinging to a familiar idea
Without questioning its background-
Is this truly conventional wisdom?

The stories we tell ourselves help
Us to live in a less ambiguous world
Where we desperately try to fit in.

We also have intractable truths
Blaring without provocation
No matter how we tiptoe around them.

The Torah standing the test of time
Provided us with the Shema where man
May merge with the all-knowing יהוה

Jesus, who came to earth for all to
Get a glimpse of and trust in a faithful
Father who guided his every thought.

Faith need not be an intellectual activity.
It is born out of a quest for an inward
"Knowing" of the deepest realities.

Contemplative prayer unites us with
Something greater than we are
Outside a circle of cleverness.

Things can be understood in multiple
Ways to envision why we are here.
You don't always have to choose one.

Ambivalence is seldom not caring.
Conflicting feelings may be warranted
When many sides of an issue are correct.

Moral codes need not be judgmental.
Compassion may override expositions.
No one can walk another's path.

Fairness is seldom evident
When criticizing others' beliefs.
Justice will be served to all who judge.

The key is respecting many angles,
The various textures of omni*science*
With Absolute within a sphere of science.

When we let go of the need to be right,
Are satisfied with supplication and
Gratitude to a God whose description is in
The eye of the beholder,
Then, most likely, will our thankfulness be
Heard by One who enjoys the praise
For what's been provided without asking.

We are then tuned into God's Voice
Which reverberates from the primordial to
The ends of the earth and beyond.
When it speaks to our heart, we
Act on it, no questions need be asked.

When we listen without ceasing, and
Notice how simple reflections repeat
With a convincing tone, the subtle
Nudges become crystal clear.
Act on them and most likely
Certainty will rise out of Ambiguity.

Childhood

By Jane A Lenzen

It was the mid 1950's and I am
Just back from recess,
A balmy Florida morning so sweet.
Mrs. Hagar, our plump, steely-eyed
Third grade teacher,
Interrupts my gaze of palm trees swaying
And the memory of recent fun on an old
Merry-Go-Round and monkey bars.

An accusing squinted stare focuses on me -
No! No! Not again.
I'm as guiltless as the wind, yet
The paddle presents anyway.
Her inward rage requires a release.

I endure blows without resistance
Classmates' young innocent eyes widen,
Each one's fear seems greater than mine,
Especially the real culprit in the room!
Yet their concerned glances comfort me.

A sacrificial lamb is required
To appease our teacher's fury.
Ah, it's over. She seems better now
As do my classmates and I......
For now anyway.
....

Kids of today have a bigger voice.
They speak louder and clearer
With a spark that isn't easily extinguished.
Many feel little fear of retribution since
they've already outsmarted most adults.
No need for shyness or bullying since
they're neurologically gifted to some
extent, unless Social Media is taken too
seriously which is, unfortunately, common.

This Alpha Generation was ushered in on
The hip of a new century where they
Talk to a smartphone like it was the
Ear of a proud mother whose name is Siri.

No matter. Give them space and watch
them run with their ingrained knowledge
of AI and VR integrated seamlessly into
their instincts, encouraged by their
Millennial parents who paved the way
toward these continuously emerging
technologies.

Now, a little advice from an old fogey:

Get outside! Run, play, climb a tree, shoot hoops, ride your bike, hopscotch, skate, jump rope, make funny faces, sing out loud…. enjoy simple silliness as a part of your day.
In essence: BE A KID!

And parents: FOSTER YOUR OFFSPRING'S FLAIR FOR FUN!!

(How's that for alliteration…)

Meditation

By Jane A Lenzen

Something akin to sleep
But it's not.
Thinking is accepted
When the mind insists.
Yet glimpses of space
Yield insights so brief.

Primal consciousness
Ours since birth
Kindled through solitude
Bereft of discontent.
Stealing quiet moments
For a return to essence.

Sangfroid heightens equanimity
Composure under difficulty
Remain cool under heat.
Pain and comfort blurred
When quiet creates
Opportunity to deepen practice.
Facades crumble
Revealing authenticity
Nothing need be different
History and future woven together.

Thoughts of better beyond
Gently interrupted by what is.
Alpha waves assume position
Calm creativity enhanced.

Sorrows blend in with silence
When a bird's song barely discernible
Penetrates the deafness
To deepen transcendence.

Nothing suppressed yields
Wild sensations and imaginings
Eventually dimmed
Within the sanctuary of zen.

Forgotten Kids

By Jane A Lenzen

Don't touch the shiny object
Color within the lines
You ask such silly questions
Quit whining and go outside
It's not that hot, go play with the dog
You're 3 years old, act like it
Do you want a spanking?
Now STOP IT!

Time to go to the store
C'mon and get in the car
Quit complaining cry baby
I'll be right back.
Oh, my gosh
The time just flew by and....
Jenny, Jenny, Jenny.......
Wake up, wake up, please......

****

Every year between 650,000 - 700,000 children are KNOWN victims of child abuse in the US. Over 4 million referrals are made per year to Child Protective Services.

Every single day, in the US, 5 children die from abuse or neglect usually at the hands of one or both parents.
Every single day......

Most of those who survive will perpetuate the abuse.

It is the most important issue facing society today but seldom discussed in the media or in the political arena.

Mini Legacy

By Jane A Lenzen

I want everyday life decisions
Not to add more burden
To a fragile world engulfed in survival.

Living life is really quite simple -
Be the person you want others to be
Greatness comes from authenticity.

Take the time to live a day in
Someone else's shoes.
Notice their frustrations then be
The one who takes an interest.

Big differences from such little effort
Expecting absolutely nothing in return.
Encouraging someone to take a risk
Because you see something they don't.
Build confidence and add to their spirit
With small ideas and bigger deeds.

Expectation of great rewards?
There should be no thought of a legacy
Because you're too busy living one.
When you die, a very tiny hole is left
To be enlarged by someone else.

All of which means, a legacy is
Meaningless
You can't really leave a legacy -
You can only BE one.

Errors of Perfection

By Jane A Lenzen

The unknowing of future events
Has guided living
In a direction toward perfection

Inquiry meets meaning when
Silence drowns out the noise
Of confusion and negativity

Keeping the mind counseled
With effort toward non-doing-
Floating atop an emerald ocean

Rough seas bring thoughts
Toward the stillness of its floor
Swaying to and fro in rhythm

Yet, mistakes made that day
Lead to misconceived excursions…
A frustrated plane of existence

Fly high to approach perfect prisms
Like a hawk soaring through the wind
Of errors toward a life well lived

Achieving perfection is not key
The art of living is.
Insistent intertwining of moments
Are all that exists.
Perfecting daily errors through
Union with unseen forces

Walk a sandy path to gentle waves
Creating a weblike lace of foam
On a shore of bursting bubbles paying
Homage to the sensual salty air

Breathe it all in knowing that minor
Errors made that day are made perfect
By these moments of unrivaled perfection

Diastolic Moments

By Jane A Lenzen

Pressure inside arteries between each
HEARTBEAT causes a momentary lull,
A slight relief for the heart, with
Rhythmic action at its lowest point.
Pumping stops, chambers become full.
An EXHALATION finds a pause before
The next inhalation begins.
A moment of pure stillness and peace
Easily lost without quiet moments,
Yet occurs in the midst of chaos.

A gaze quickens to a stare
Which then must BLINK.
This moment of non-looking
Does not hamper the
Observation of the subject.

These infinitesimal fleeting moments
Provide tiny bits of knowledge into the
Art of a meditative state.
Glimpses that light up the mind
To possibilities seldom witnessed.

A PENDULUM swings in a fixed position
Slowing down before
PAUSING at the end of each to and fro -
Enjoying the ease with which it moves,
The pivot point path steady and smooth.

A ball thrown up in the air "knows"
When to yield to gravity.
This HESITATION before falling back to
Earth, like a bird gliding through air, is
Effortless without irregularities.

These diastolic MOMENTS donate
Peaceful spaces without seeking,
A stillness requiring
No thought or effort.
A gift given, unnoticed.

NATURE'S NATURAL PAUSES provide
Tiny tranquil quietude all without effort.

Memories

By Jane A Lenzen

Amazing how so many memories
Are tied up in such a tiny little space.
The mighty reach of years past
Come blazing forth in time travel
Out of photo frames from this mass
We refer to as the mind within a brain.

Memories of sea against azure blue skies
Gentle waves lulling us to a place
Where the sand gently caresses
With a softening touch yielding to
Another movie of how youth need not
Rationalize how time is joyously spent.

Oh, the memories never cease
To melt away the difficult times
Where these moments of reprieve
Give recitation to words not forgotten,
The songs that easily join reverie
By a rhythmic cadence of atoms within.

The oscillation of world events
Are stilled by the memories of
Freedom and purity bearing witness
To the present resonating images
Of faces long gone whose impressions
Are embedded in appreciation and love.

Just imagine a life without memories.
Each moment of the day would be new.
No comparisons to be judged good or bad
Yet without them the journey would fail
To delight the senses with familiarity;
A life which rouses a nostalgia
Of simpler times seemingly
Without complications.

Is it possible to enjoy memorable scenes
Without yearning for the "better" days?
In reality, memories morph into a time
Where the best moments in the world
Come in the form of a simple hug from
Your child. Does any time in youth even
Come close?

Let's view these mental movies
Through today's youthful eyes ready to
Grab the world by the tail towards a
Bright future and exciting adventures,
With much much more to come…..

Where they eventually rush towards an
Age of Grateful Reminiscing.

And so goes the circle of life…..

Mythical Truths
By Jane A Lenzen

Stories of old teach us new lessons
Passed down from generations.
People struggled since the beginning
To make sense of a world they
Continually want to change.

If humans could learn from history
The unbounded raw experiences,
Take a moment and gaze deeper
Into the Roundabout of it all….
How much we change into sameness.

The identical magical stars, which
Guided ocean explorers centuries ago
Through travels of treacherous waves,
Still astound those who now cruise
Rough waters with casual ease
To blissful drifts swaying toward
Vast symphonies of a perfect pitch.

Like ocean travelers, this adventure into
Revered ideas of old bring forth an ache
And yearning for understanding beyond
The ideas that have floated around
For centuries on end.

Omnivalent sacred legends can
Generate symbols of hope and truth.
Listen well and follow altruistic ways
To avoid the tendency for superiority
Which strangles the soul.

Societies past and present all engender a
Golden Calf when facing times of
Wilderness, that vast emptiness inside
That money, people, stuff, drugs and
Prestige cannot pacify.

We eventually turn to that which is real-
Sacred encounters revealing epiphanies
Which surrender to the Mind of God.
Universal principles are all inclusive
Guiding us on an infinite path where the
Supernatural can melt snow
Through a simple laser like gaze
Allowing the traveler an easier trek.

Whether ancient texts are authentic or
Not does not matter one bit.
Our affinity for immortal sacredness
Is held with a tenacious grip,
Letting go at the end
To a joyful Beginning.

The Beach

By Jane A Lenzen

It's another sunny day waiting to burn

flesh of teenagers hell-bent on having

the whitest teeth and darkest tan around.

The pavilion permeates aromas of half
burnt hamburgers and french fries, salted
to perfection enticing the young to spend
their hard-earned change from odd
summer jobs.

Seagulls know we will share since we're All
Rightful Residents of the same island.

It's the mid 20th century. Wasting food,
considered a sin, was assuaged with the
flinging in the air of leftover buns and fries
met with hungry eager beaks.

Volleyball in the sugar white sand, chicken
fights in the salty gulf, colorful beach balls
tossed around like hot potatoes…..

Live music from a local band playing from
the rooftop pavilion where ivory blooms
on sea grapes can be seen for miles. One
quarter, hand stamped, and up the stairs
you go for Barefoot Dancing until the sweat
reminds you to take another swim.

Racing into the water, a few dare to swim
to the first sand bar, which seems miles

away. Arriving exhausted, we stand up
and wave to those back on shore. Then an
urge wells up in me to spontaneously swim
further to the next sandbar.

Dolphins beckon me to go with them
so how can I refuse? Once there, people
appear as little miniature dolls sitting on
chairs under colorful umbrellas. It feels like
being in the middle of the sea, away from
anything that smacked of humanity.

I could live out here forever and don't want
to swim back. This panorama of green
belongs to me. I dive into it, encouraging
sea creatures to swim closer and sure
enough, they oblige.

The waves spring forth in a rhythmic surge
beckoning me to jump through Poseidon
perfection. The salt water mirroring the
fluid running through my veins, runs up my
nose with a familiar sting. Dolphins decide
to curiously surface, studying this aquatic
human who seems far from home. I am one
with this Gulf that Gifts me with exquisite
sea creatures who play with this being so
vastly unique from them.

Time to leave. I am lucky again and beat
the pulling undertow by swimming mostly
parallel back to shore. Once my feet touch
bottom I slide each step into the sand to

avoid surprising a stingray. The few jellyfish I meet, graciously allow me to pass without tentacles touching my youthful skin. Riding a wave back to shore, I rise up out of the gulf with exhilaration.

Another day at the beach - sunburned, salty, sandy, joyful and carefree.

Nothing feels separate from me.

I am part of the Beach's Pulse…..its every wave crashing towards the shoreline with a predicted rhythm of which I am a part

and will be

Forever.

Printed in the United States
by Baker & Taylor Publisher Services